Gallery Books
Editor: Peter Fallon

KING OF THE CASTLE

By the same author

Stage plays produced
    Breakdown
    Swift
    Pull Down a Horseman
    Some Women on the Island

Television plays
    A Matter of Conscience
    The Funeral
    Cancer ⎫
    Heritage ⎬ *A trilogy dealing with contemporary Ulster*
    Siege ⎭

Books
    Victims, a novel
    Heritage and Other Stories

Eugene McCabe

King of the Castle

Eugene McCabe

Gallery Books

King of the Castle is published simultaneously in paperback and in a clothbound, limited edition of 250 copies signed by the author, by
The Gallery Press
19 Oakdown Road
Dublin 14. Ireland.

ISBN 0 902996 70 3 (*clothbound*)
0 902996 71 1 (*paperback*)

The Gallery Press gratefully acknowledges the assistance of An Chomhairle Ealaíon (The Arts Council of Ireland) towards the publication of this book.

Applications for a licence to perform this play by Professional or Amateur Companies must be made in advance to the Gallery Press.

King of the Castle

A play in Two Acts

King of the Castle received the Irish Life Award in 1964 and was first produced on the 2nd of September in that year at The Gaiety Theatre, Dublin, with the following players:

Scober (Barney) MacAdam	Martin Dempsey
Tressa	Pauline Delaney
Matt Lynch	T. P. McKenna
Jemmy Maguire	John Cowley
Joady Conlon	Brian O'Higgins
Old Jim Hughes	Dermot McDowell
Tommy Hayes	Kevin Redmond
Charlie Tobin	Des Nealon
Pete Duggan	John McMahon
Ned O'Meara	Edward Byrne
Larry Maguire	Vincent Smith
Liam Conlon	William Brady
Direction	Godfrey Quigley
Design	William McCrow
Lighting	Paddy O'Toole

*For Ruth, Marcus,
Patrick and Stephen*

Characters

Scober (Barney) MacAdam, the King
Tressa, his wife
Matt Lynch, a travelling thresherman
Jemmy Maguire, a small farmer
Joady Conlon, a small farmer
Old Jim Hughes, a small farmer
Tommy Hayes, a small farmer
Charlie Tobin, publican and storekeeper
Bridie Hagerty, a maidservant
Ned O'Meara, a farm worker
Larry Maguire, Jemmy's son
Liam Conlon, Joady's son

Place: a Leitrim farm, Clonhaggard
Time: the late 1950s.

ACT ONE

*Early evening. The yard of Clonhaggard. The threshing is nearing
its end for the day—but the yard is full of activity. Bags, bales and
weighing scales on stage. Stony upland fields beyond.*

> CONLON *and* MAGUIRE *front stage are weighing
> and tying the bags of threshed corn.* CONLON *shows*
> MAGUIRE *a handful of the seed.*

CONLON   Well?! Not bad for the mountain!

MAGUIRE   S'alright.

> LYNCH *now leaves* SCOBER *to tend the bags and
> comes over from the mill to check the pile of bags
> on the trolley behind* MAGUIRE *and* CONLON.

CONLON   There's a lot of it.

LYNCH   A good start. *(He goes on counting.* LYNCH
glances around at the mountain scrub land.)

CONLON   You never threshed here before?

> LYNCH *shakes his head still counting.*

LYNCH   Balincomer West . . . that was my run.

MAGUIRE   Was?

LYNCH   This week I quit.

MAGUIRE   For where?

LYNCH   Canada.

MAGUIRE   You're one of the Killgorm Lynches . . .?

LYNCH   That's right.

MAGUIRE   Sold out . . . a year back?

> LYNCH *nods.*

LYNCH   And you?

MAGUIRE   Maguire . . . Jemmy . . . neighbour to Joady
here . . . and the man who hired you: Scober
MacAdam.

LYNCH   Where's all this land?

MAGUIRE   Scober can grow stuff on rocks . . . he does it to
shame his neighbours.

> LYNCH *looks around at the house and yard.*

LYNCH   He's spent some money; last time I passed it was ready to fall.

MAGUIRE   *(jerking his head in* SCOBER'S *direction)* Let no man live bar himself: watch the neighbours die, and when they're buried . . . he can buy.

CONLON   Aye, but for what.

MAGUIRE   For what is right! . . . See that cub at the straps . . .

CONLON   Larry?

MAGUIRE   An' your son Liam — some day they'll carry us through a door feet first . . . but when the hump is sunk and the stone side-ways, they'll walk a rocky bounds we've clawed since God knows when . . . Blood . . . Sons! . . . *(Jerking his thumb at* SCOBER*)* What'll he leave? A sour dry tit!

TRESSA *comes on stage, and pauses, looking at the threshing activities, waiting to catch* SCOBER'S *eye.* CONLON *nudges* MAGUIRE, *and they both stare, lecherously, smiling. As* SCOBER *has not noticed her, she goes up to them.*

TRESSA   It's ready.

MAGUIRE   What?

TRESSA *takes note of, but ignores the insolence . . . She watches for another moment.*

TRESSA   Tell them . . . *(She exits towards the house.)*

CONLON   Broody and sour, eh? If the right man got at her for a night she'd sweeten . . .

MAGUIRE   Maybe . . . 'cause money won't. Her first year here, he bought for her like gentry . . . painted, stripped, re-floored from top to bottom — gadgets, fancy furniture . . . what not . . . from a man who lived in one room for twenty years . . . with a paraffin stove, and orange boxes . . . but the moneymoon's gone sour. I pass late . . . I've seen them. Take a man, anywhere, Joady, a trier like Scober . . . he'd made money . . . or was born to it . . . hammered out a name for himself, a business, a farm, or a family, . . . he's this, that, the other . . . you know how they talk when a man makes money . . . and watch him . . . watch him hard . . . and some day, some night, you'll get him naked . . . and he's nothin'! A child bangin' his fist on the wall.

CONLON   I've heard them too . . . they shout.

MAGUIRE   He took on a young man's job: it's not every buck'll please a girl—but when they lie with Scober's age, and no results . . . they start to think it's rationed out to them — and get this hungry look.

CONLON   Aye . . .

CONLON makes a motion of eating and drinking, and as they start to move offstage, LYNCH gives the direction, and the hum of the motor begins to fade. The rest of the men come offstage, palming sweat from their eyes, dusting their caps, and clothes, and moving across the stage slowly.
Drop down or draw back on the hall set:
A heavy table, lengthways facing the audience, is set for about twelve men: TRESSA has just finished laying cutlery; she checks it, and then goes to a window, stares a while, and then moves towards the kitchen door. MAGUIRE and CONLON come in, MAGUIRE taking off his cap and pulling the lank strands into position across his narrow white pate. CONLON stuffs his beret into his pocket and runs a hand through his dense crinkles. They both nod at TRESSA, watching her, and then mutter:

"Mam" and " 'Lo Mam".

TRESSA   Anywhere you like.

They move towards the two seats near the audience.

MAGUIRE   *(watching her closely)* Warm . . .

TRESSA   The rest . . . are they . . .?

CONLON   On their way . . .

MAGUIRE   *(Generally)* A good yield of stuff out there . . .

CONLON   There is . . .

MAGUIRE   *(To TRESSA)* Put a belly on your lofts.

TRESSA moves to the kitchen door, saying something

inaudible. Sound of voices and footsteps approaching the hall door. A dozen men or so come in, pulling off their caps and berets. Some carry their jackets or army jerkins. LYNCH *and* SCOBER *come in last and take the two seats nearest the door.* SCOBER *is at the head of the table. He takes off his hat and runs his hand nervously through his cropped hair . . . his face expressionless.* TRESSA *carries in plates of meat and bread on a tray and begins to serve the men. The men begin eating.*

MAGUIRE   Looks a good yield, Scober.
LYNCH   Good as I've threshed this year . . . or any other.

Murmur of general approval, nods etc., followed by a scraping, clatter and chewing of eaters: TRESSA *comes in again with a bowl of lettuce and a plate of hard boiled eggs.*

   Useful bitch I saw in the yard.
SCOBER   She works well.
LYNCH   Scotch collie?
SCOBER   She is.
MAGUIRE   Get the dog yet?
SCOBER   Twice.
MAGUIRE   Pups?
SCOBER   *(Nodding)* Aye.
MAGUIRE   She's a well made bitch alright—fast—I've seen her work.
SCOBER   Clever.
MAGUIRE   How about a pup next time, Scober?

There is a noticeable pause.

SCOBER   *(Woodenly)* If you want to buy.

Pause.

MAGUIRE   I'll buy.

Pause.

SCOBER   She's not local bred . . . came out of Scotland . . . cost me 200 guineas . . . I'd need twenty pounds for a pup.

14

MAGUIRE	*(Drily)* You'll not get twenty pounds in this country, maybe not twenty shillings.

Murmur of agreement.

SCOBER	Not in *this* country . . .
MAGUIRE	The other litters . . . what'd you get?
SCOBER	For any I sold . . . £20.
MAGUIRE	The ones you didn't?
SCOBER	I drowned.
MAGUIRE	*(Muttered)* Christ!

An exchange of looks.

LYNCH	*(Smiling)* You're a businessman, Scober . . .
MAGUIRE	That makes it sound nice.

Pause: more eating, scraping of plates, handing about of bread etc.

OLD JIM HUGHES	You'll go to Drumkieran, Scober . . .?

SCOBER *nods.*

CONLON	To buy, or sell?
SCOBER	Both.
MAGUIRE	You know what'd pay well as anythin' in this country? *(Pause)* Women . . .

A few chuckles, and the men elbow each other.

Aye . . . *(Pause)* A lorry load of women . . . that's what you'd get profit on.

More laughter, winking, nodding, and elbowing.

ANOTHER WORKER	That's a fact, Jemmy . . . they're scarce about here.

SCOBER *nods with a bleak smile.*

CONLON	You'd get customers alright . . . there's only five men at this table have a woman.

TOMMY HAYES	To theirselves . . .
	Laughter.
MAGUIRE	They hope.

More laughter.

TOMMY HAYES, *a large, balding, innocent looking man, laughs louder and longer than the rest. He has a thick, spluttering laugh.*

	I'd say, Tommy, you'd take one—am I right?
TOMMY HAYES	On trial . . . *(he bursts out laughing).*
ANOTHER	
WORKER	You'll burn for that, Tommy.
CONLON	You'll not get one too handy on trial—they like the bit of gold on the finger.
MAGUIRE	There's plenty of men can get them without that . . . and other ways.
TOMMY HAYES	You get a dog on trial . . . why not a woman? *(He roars laughing again.)*
CONLON	You want the right breedy woman—and a worker—a woman there that can milk a cow, dress a pig, bake bread and keep house—all this squealin' and buckleppin' in dance halls has them like mares ahorsin' . . . and the country full o' stallions . . .
MAGUIRE	*(Quietly)* There's an odd gelding . . .

Pause, and smile. SCOBER *faintly reacts.*

	(To HAYES*)* Hasn't Phelan there beside you—a lump of a daughter, Tommy—you should go up an odd night and dig his garden.
TOMMY HAYES	Aggie Phelan, she's got a beard.

Laughter.

MAGUIRE	A bit a hair about the chin—what harm'll that do *her* or *you*?
TOMMY HAYES	I'll wait for something sweeter.
OLD JIM HUGHES	'Till you're my go—fit for nothin'—but buckets and talk with sheep dogs—there's too many that way . . .

MAGUIRE *(To* CONLON*)* There's men has them doesn't make much of them.

Sudden silence . . . MAGUIRE, *smiling, lifts a plate of hard boiled eggs.*

LYNCH Eggs here, did you get wan, Scober? We have them down here.

MAGUIRE *looks at* CONLON *and smiles, and the eggs are passed around their end of the table.*

MAGUIRE I like an odd egg.
LYNCH *(Politely trying to break the tension)* Is it ewes tomorrow at Drumkieran?

SCOBER *nods.*

SCOBER I've three rams to buy.
LYNCH Lambs or two year olds?
SCOBER I like the older ram.
MAGUIRE Never trust an auld ram, Scober—what do you say, Joady?
CONLON Chancy.
MAGUIRE You could end up with a mountain of empty sheep. The auld ram . . . he'll sniff, but there doesn't be the same kick about him . . . for a crop of lambs.

SCOBER *shrugs his contempt.*

OLD JIM HUGHES *(Without implication)* Lamb rams or auld rams . . . the wool should be clipped off the ewe's behind . . . what d'ye say, men?

Simultaneous murmurs for and against:

A good job, Jim.
No call for it.
Loss of time.
It helps.
Cod.

17

OLD JIM HUGHES   We're all sheepmen here . . . I say, off with the wool, give the ram a chance.

MAGUIRE   I'd an Inspector called last week . . . one of these boys with a Volks, and a government face . . . "You supply the bottling plant at Kilmacthomas" says he . . . *(Pause)* "Me and some other men", says I, "I've only two cows . . ."

Laughter.

"Have ye them cows clipped", says he . . . *(Pause)* "We don't clip cows up this way", says I . . . "The udder", says he—very dry—"you'll have to clip the hair off the udder—it's cleaner.

Long pause: CONLON *gives a peal of laughter in anticipation:* MAGUIRES *stares at him woodenly, with a clowning expression.*

"How would you lek", says I, "to be out on this mountain in the middle of January, and the hair clipped off your udder? . . .

They all laugh loudly, nudging each other: LYNCH *also laughs; again* SCOBER *smiles bleakly.*

SIMULTANEOUSLY   You're an awful man, Jemmy . . .
Christ, that's a terror . . .
Oh! He said it!
He's a fright to the world . . .

Pause.

TOMMY HAYES   What'd he say then, Jemmy?

MAGUIRE   Went off very cut . . . "get that done" he said—bad bugger—lek all those government men—tramp over you; get fat on the bribes the big fellas give them.

TRESSA *comes in with a crock of apples, followed by* BRIDIE: *who puts a large pot of tea on the table and exits.*

If you've a walled-in garden and fat, well watered land, you just say "Ah! Mr. Hannigan, just in time for coffee." *(Pause)* Then they have their coffee and maybe a shot of whiskey in it—and the bad bugger says "Everythin' in order, I suppose."

TRESSA puts the apples on the table and nods towards some of the men.

OLD JIM HUGHES   I remarked those from the haggard.
CONLON   They yield well.
TOMMY HAYES   Best ever I seen.

Some men reach for the apples, MAGUIRE *takes one and bites it.*

MAGUIRE   Clean, sharp, sweet. How does it come you get this big crop, Scober? *(Pause)* Bit of shelter maybe?
OLD JIM HUGHES   There was no walls any good to that frost in May.
MAGUIRE   I know what he done . . . Don't I, Scober?

Pause.

He'd stay up every night of Spring, wouldn't you Scober . . . *(Pause)* for the right crop. *(Winks at* CONLON*)* I twigged him one Spring night—on my way home. The back of this place was all lit up, sparks in the frost; tar barrels along one side of the orchard—and this black figure of a man—in and out through the trees, with arms of straw. "Christ", says I, "am I dead, in hell . . . or what?" *(Pause)* Am I right, Scober?

SCOBER stares.

When other men sleep, Scober bes up all night, thinkin' of his apples in September. Am I right, Scober?

There is a muttered comment and the cruching of apples.

MAGUIRE   *(To his son, beside him, catching at his sleeve)*
          Never waste the butt of an apple son, the butt
          with the seed—that's the whole secret—am I
          right, Scober?
SCOBER   *(Drily)* So *they* say.

          *TRESSA has gone here and there refilling the large
          mugs with tea, hot from the kitchen; and, self-
          conscious, she moves from man to man, nodding,
          saying quietly:*

TRESSA   That alright? . . . Enough? . . .

          *Aware of the approving and lecherous eyes which
          follow her, she is about to move away from the
          table when MAGUIRE calls to her:*

MAGUIRE   Is there another drop there, woman? . . . If you
          please . . .

          *She goes to him and begins pouring: he looks up
          at her.*

TRESSA   All right?
MAGUIRE   Do well . . .

          *SCOBER, listening with half an ear to LYNCH and
          the old man, has been watching her with MAGUIRE.
          He crooks a forefinger towards her; she goes up
          to him and pours into his mug. Unlike the other
          men, he watches the mug filling and not her. When
          it is full, he nods.*

          You'll pit those apples, Scober?
SCOBER   *(With cold hatred)* Doesn't keep rats out.
MAGUIRE   The hay lofts?
SCOBER   They get dried up.
MAGUIRE   *(Smiling at CONLON)* A bad job that . . .

          Pause.

CONLON   Where do you store them, Scober?

Pause, while SCOBER *continues staring at* MAGUIRE.

MAGUIRE Joady asked—where do you store them? . . .
SCOBER I sell them.
MAGUIRE *(Pontificating)* There's only one way of storin'
apples—Nature's way.

TRESSA, *who is pouring for another man, pauses to
listen.*

The grass round my apple trees is rank and when
an apple falls it gets buried: birds don't see it—
rats don't guess—childer miss it and it lies there—
free of frost and damp, against the ground. Last
March I turned in fresh lambed ewes one morning,
at duskus I gathered a bag of apples—firm and
sharp—sweet as the September day they fell . . .

Simultaneous comment:

Damn but —
I'd believe it.
Aye, it's true.
SCOBER *(Mutters something to* LYNCH*).*
MAGUIRE Am I right, Scober?
SCOBER A bag!
MAGUIRE Full . . .

*They stare at each other, down the table, and
during a momentary uneasy pause:*

MAGUIRE *(To* TRESSA*)* Sweet as the September day they fell.
SCOBER *(Still staring at* MAGUIRE: *points a vicious fore-
finger down the table)* . . . Sugar . . .

*Two or three men reach urgently for the sugar,
and it is passed to* SCOBER. *He puts three or four
spoons in his mug and stirs. The threshermen
watch hypnotically as though seeing a ritual:*
TRESSA *goes down with the tea pot. The light
outside is gold, and in the hall now it is half-light.
Long pause: more eating: drinking of tea etc.*

OLD JIM HUGHES MURMURS	I see poor Halpin's in the "Celt", Scober . . . Pity of him.
	Poor fella.
	The head went.
OLD JIM HUGHES	A man with childer and roots in the mountain— no sense to it . . . *(Pause)* What made him do thon?
MAGUIRE	Bad luck, since his woman died, a dose of sheep got braxy—the thatch rotted and fell in on him— his corn lodged and all the crows in Ireland lit on it—poor fella, used to run out half mad, with sticks and shouts—put up that many scarecrows, he looked like one himself . . . in the end.
TOMMY HAYES	Not a damn bit of good once they get the notion.
CONLON	When his roan cow calved wrong—the head went.
MAGUIRE	It's been gone since he buried her . . . *(Pause)* Childer cryin' at night.
CONLON	Drowned himself in a bog hole.
SCOBER	*(Coldly factual)* He wouldn't help himself . . . he was the bad luck type.

Pause, as some of the men exchange glances.

MAGUIRE	I suppose you'll buy, Scober?
SCOBER	His land lies into yours—maybe you'll buy?
MAGUIRE	*(Loudly)* Me buy—with what?!
SCOBER	*(Shrugging)* A bag of apples? Sweet as the September day they fell . . .?

As the men smile, MAGUIRE *is seen to mouth a curse.*

SCOBER	*(Pleased)* What's that? —
MAGUIRE	A title for you, Scober—you haven't earned it . . .
SCOBER	Every man earns his own way . . .
MAGUIRE	*(More to the table than to* SCOBER*)* Twenty—fifty years from now, when crows come to lodged corn—you'll have Maguires, Tobins, Hagertys, Halpins, Conlons, poor little raggy men with sticks—who'll run and shout and talk with grippers, bury the last cow—break roots, work

in British tunnels, live in kip houses, and when they've suffered—come back . . .

SCOBER *(Quietly and drily)* And drown themselves in a bog-hole.

Pause: MAGUIRE *and* SCOBER *stare tensely at each other.*

MAGUIRE *(Loudly)* The paper says the late Michael Halpin *is survived* by his two sons—John and Peter Halpin.

Pause.

LYNCH Alright — alright . . .
SCOBER *(Very tense)* I'd prefer open talk to riddles—let the man talk—maybe you'd like to stand.
MAGUIRE I can stand alright. How about you, Scober?

Pause.

LYNCH *(Arbitrating and getting to his feet)* Can we move from here . . .

The threshermen all murmur agreement and stand up, pushing back their chairs, half of them blessing themselves: caps and berets pulled from knees and put on: last mouthfuls of tea being swallowed. SCOBER *and* MAGUIRE *remain seated . . .* SCOBER *rising first:*

SCOBER Tobins?

There is general murmur, and smiles.

ALL I'll not say no.
Who's payin?
Surely.
What time is it?
Why not?
It'll clear the auld wind pipe.

CONLON *(To* MAGUIRE, *who is still seated, brooding)* . . .
What about Jemmy . . .

MAGUIRE I've *work* to do . . . Later—maybe.

SCOBER *stares, about to say something.*

OLD JIM HUGHES Could you run me home first, Scober . . .?

SCOBER Surely Jim . . . or any man *has work* of his own.

A couple of other small farmers nod and SCOBER *nods back. They file out the door,* SCOBER *in the middle of them.*

SCOBER *(Offstage)* I'll be about . . . *(Pause)* half an hour.

VOICE We'll keep room for your round.

Laughter and talk offstage as the motor starts. As the last man goes out MAGUIRE *puts his cap on the seat beside him. He then moves towards the door as* TRESSA *comes onstage from the kitchen.* MAGUIRE *pauses at the door, looking at the men outside and then back to* TRESSA *who has begun clearing the table.*

MAGUIRE That was good grub, Missus . . .

TRESSA *nods at him. He hesitates, looking at her and then goes.* TRESSA *goes to the window and looks out: as she does,* MAGUIRE *appears again.*

MAGUIRE *(Pointing)* Cap . . .

TRESSA *goes to where he was sitting, gets the cap and hands it to him. He hesitates, half smiling, and then takes it, examining it.*

Way out there—in the cold parts, some men wear 'em with fur . . . Fur on the outside—wouldn't care much about it—what'd you say?

Pause.

TRESSA I don't know.

MAGUIRE   I don't lek it . . . fur on man or woman—
          redickullus—looks like animals—clipped and
          clean—that's the way I like things . . .

          Pause. TRESSA *is watching him carefully.*

          I seen a fella once in London, one winter—a mad
          frigger in a sun hat—and a fur coat—fur as thick
          as that—and it down to his ankles—God's truth
          —and he had them tennis shoes on—'course he
          was mad . . . *(Pause)* Underground—Tottenham
          Court Road, no man passed any remarks on him
          —but Jemmy here from the mountain—I stared
          after him—"You're a mad frigger" I said; he
          didn't hear me . . . *(Pause)* 'Course it's a big
          town . . . *(Pause)* Bar Dublin you never been in
          a big town?

          Long pause.

TRESSA   No.

          Longer pause.

MAGUIRE   Lonesome places—big cities—more lonesome'n
          the mountain . . . *(Pause)* Less you've a family . . .

          TRESSA *looks bored.*

          You want the family . . .

          TRESSA *mutters something.*

MAGUIRE   *(With a slight change of tone)* What'd ye say?

          TRESSA *shakes her head.*

          What?
TRESSA   Nothing—I said nothing.
MAGUIRE   You must've said somethin' — *(Pause)* 'Scuse
          me daughter, but you did—'cos I said "You want
          the family" and then you said something—I

25

couldn't catch—quietly, under your skirt like . . .

TRESSA *(Moves away)* You've got your cap—I've work to do.

MAGUIRE I could give a hand . . .

TRESSA It's all right.

Pause.

MAGUIRE *(Grins at her)* Does Scober give you the hand *(Pause)* I seen you—one night . . . *(he grins and winks, pointing at the mirror nodding)* Yeah . . . *(he cups his hands against his chest)* Am I right? Eh! We know somethin' . . . don't we, daughter— me and you—am I right? . . . me an' Scober, we were cubs together; that's right—you're startin' hard—lek a woman not too happy at her work— eh. *(Pause; moving away)* Line up fifty women, and Jemmy knows—this one has a man, this one has a knuck—this one has a money-makin' rig. Ever ass yourself—what a woman's for?—Scrape plates, twig floors—look at rocks and heather, eat, cook, sleep, drink, empty pots, feed men— and hens, talk with a hired girl, confess on Saturday, pray of a Sunday, and think of sin all day Monday? That what she's for? Keepin' her belly full and the pots empty? *(He has moved a little closer: intensely:)* No! What so?

TRESSA *has backed away, fascinated and disgusted.*

To drain a man—make a chile—and rear a man. *(Pause)* 'Less she does that—she's fat—good for nothing, but walkin' about, chewin' her cud, — empty— a loss . . .

TRESSA *(Quietly)* Get out . . .

MAGUIRE *(Casually)* Takes a smart man to live in kip houses—and keep his money, his health and his woman happy . . .

Pause.

TRESSA *(Alert)* What man?

MAGUIRE	Any man.
TRESSA	Barney?
MAGUIRE	Scober's one man . . . *(Pause)* Ever remark him when the crack's high—he'll smile and stare, and when it's dull he'll laugh—at nothin'. Poor sign of a man that—no nature . . .

TRESSA *stares unlistening.*

TRESSA	What kip houses—where?
MAGUIRE	Big towns anywhere—he travelled a lot—still does . . .
TRESSA	*(Quietly)* You're a liar.
MAGUIRE	I seen him.
TRESSA	*(Mimicking)* You . . . seen?
MAGUIRE	That's right.
TRESSA	Where? When?
MAGUIRE	Years back . . .
TRESSA	*(Quietly)* With a woman?
MAGUIRE	There was a woman there—but he was like always —in a corner, smilin'—at the glass of whiskey— not the woman. *(He taps his head.)* Same then as now—greed—and the fixed notion—it burns a man up—till he's good for nothin' . . .

TRESSA *thumbs towards the door.* MAGUIRE *ignores her.*

MAGUIRE	Am I right?
TRESSA	You're smaller than he says.
MAGUIRE	My son's bigger than he can stomach.
TRESSA	*(Louder)* Get out . . . Out . . .

MAGUIRE *moves towards the door still looking at* TRESSA *with cunning insolence.*

MAGUIRE	Empty—a loss—but that's up to you—if he's away—and you want service with profit—Jemmy can oblige anytime—with pleasure.

MAGUIRE *goes:* TRESSA *goes to the bedroom . . . and changes for bed, opens a drawer and takes out*

27

knitting, grows impatient with it: gets a magazine and leafs tensely through it, waiting for SCOBER. *When he comes in he glances at her: she does not look up and he goes to a small table with a lamp on it and begins rooting in his pockets. He takes out a wad of notes, removes an elastic band and counts the notes intently. He replaces the elastic band and returns the wad to his pocket. He then counts coins which he roots out of other pockets.*

TRESSA   You were a while, Barney?

SCOBER   Had to run Jim over to Boolawater.

TRESSA   I heard rain . . .

SCOBER   He's still got hay cocked along the river . . . Lammas floods on the way . . . can't understand a man like that.

TRESSA   He's a bachelor . . . nothing to work for.

SCOBER   I was a long time a bachelor.

TRESSA *goes back to the magazine.*

SCOBER   What's in that?

TRESSA   It tells about lace making . . . there's a book about it.

SCLBER   You should get that, daughter.

TRESSA   Yes.

SCOBER   Dropped into Tobins on the way back . . . cost me a couple of quid. They were all there but the boys I left home.

TRESSA   Maguire?

SCOBER   He didn't show. He was half-cut anyway.

TRESSA   He's . . .

Pause.

SCOBER   Yes?

TRESSA   An uncommon man when you're close to him.

SCOBER   You think?

TRESSA   When you see him in the house.

SCOBER   Slobbering in pubs, yahooing at the crossroads after dark . . . common I'd say . . .

Pause.

TRESSA Barney?

SCOBER Yes.

TRESSA Nothing.

SCOBER Go on, daughter . . . go on.

TRESSA Are you happy?

SCOBER Am I happy?

TRESSA Yes?

SCOBER Well?, Yes . . . most ways . . . tethered a bit maybe . . . times I'd as leif have less . . . milk a cow or two . . . up early to dig or gather the day long . . . bone tired at duskus . . . eat and drink like a horse . . . sleep sound . . . it's never that way: Rain when you wake . . . a toothache maybe or a cold . . . or your head's light from whiskey or you've been vexed from half-dark with cares . . . or up half the night at figures . . . coming or goining; docks, marts; money to make; the day never comes when you do the things you as leif do . . . it's most times things you'd as leif not do . . . *(Pause)* . . . but . . . happy? Happy I'd say as any man . . . why?

TRESSA Just.

SCOBER Just what?

TRESSA Do you love me, Barney? Please look at me . . . do you?

SCOBER You jump things on me woman . . . Am I happy? Do I love you? . . . Words, respect is better.

TRESSA I say them.

SCOBER Respect is better.

TRESSA You don't understand . . .

SCOBER Too well.

Long pause.

TRESSA He doesn't respect you.

SCOBER Who?

TRESSA Maguire.

SCOBER He's jealous—that's respect . . . jealous, 'cause I've worked—used my head—put lorries on the road—got this place and others, bought out most of the mountain—planted timber, built barns, roofed yards—I employ men—I have a young

wife ... *(Pause, pointing up)* Electric ...
(Longish pause) I was in rags at school with all
of them—but you've got to stay that way—raggy,
stupid and poor—"Ah! sure it's a hard life" and
"How can a man live where snipes starve?" "But
won't we get our reward afterwards?"—slobber!!
(Pointing out) There's ton of barley to the acre
from three inches of soil out there—stones, a lot
of it—and there's men in Meath on the fattest
land in Ireland'd lie happy with a yield like
that, and still the fools'd starve before they'd
ask "How's it done?" "Can I do it?"—Spite!
Ignorance! Envy. Let 'em starve—let 'em live on
spite and take the boat—rotten thatch with lumps
of grass—all sunk away from the chimneys—
windows that leave it dusk inside of a summer's
day—the dung heap and the bony cow—the
messy yard and the few mousey sheep—I was
born to it—know every hour of it—the waste, the
crownshawning by the fire in winter—Everything
to blame but themselves and 'cause they don't do
anything—like Maguire, they've time to watch—
every turf you save and lamb you mark—the
lorries that come and go—they count and
question and what they don't know they guess,
and if man improves—they say: "No man bests
the mountain less he's a thief like Bull Haggard".
But if you work and deal and best the mountain—
you've made *dirt* of them—and that's what they
hate—order—yields—business, the power to buy
...

TRESSA   *(Remotely)* For what?
SCOBER   Eh?!
TRESSA   I said for what?
SCOBER   How do you mean? —
TRESSA   All this buying—what's it for?

Pause.

SCOBER   Us.

Pause while SCOBER *reflects.*

30

Hundreds of years—we've scraped those rocks—
the graveyards full of McAdams—Tobins—
Mullarkeys—lived and died—lek scarcecrows.
When I was a cub I could see this place—these
windows lit up like a ship. Now I look out of
them . . .

TRESSA At neighbours . . . you've bought out—at no-
things. I'm listening now three years—you go on
and on and on, Barney—talking to yourself—
power—the mountain—spite and the neighbours
—soon we'll have no neighbours—we don't even
fit it right . . .

SCOBER We can afford it . . .

TRESSA Not enough . . .

SCOBER If you pay for a thing—you fit it.

TRESSA *(Unlistening)* Those people last week . . .

SCOBER To hell with them.

Pause.

TRESSA What I didn't say was what she said when I
opened the door. *(Pause)* I'd an apron on—she
asked—very nicely: was there *anybody* at home . . .

SCOBER *reacts with annoynace.*

So I said no . . . what could I say when they
thought I worked here. They wanted to see round
the place, the house and garden—she had spent
holidays here with her aunts—did I think the
present owners would mind? "No," I said, "it's
all right" and I went back to the kitchen.

SCOBER This means what?

TRESSA We don't fit it . . .

SCOBER An empty barracks with no roof when I got it—
laurel branches through that window there—now
look . . .

TRESSA *looks up without interest.*

TRESSA *(Pause)* It doesn't leak—it's wrong every other
way . . .

31

SCOBER *stares.*

SCOBER We've spent money on it but—it's wrong—it should be different—how?!

TRESSA Don't shout, Barney ... *(Pause)* Take our dump room off the hall, it used to be a library—the shelving's still there ... My first week here I counted how many books went round the walls *(Pause)* ... Guess ...

SCOBER *shrugs with annoyance.*

Five thousand.

SCOBER I'd prefer bank notes—you can buy bread with them ...

TRESSA That's why we've none.

SCOBER So! ...

TRESSA So—it's different now—we keep worm doses, cod liver oil, farming papers, syringes, pig powders—and twenty years of Old Moore's Almanac, where there used to be five thousands books—women in long dresses—candle light—wine—a big log fire.

SCOBER 'S not so long since we were growled at by gun dogs—and handed gruel in workhouses, those with no pride—the rest stayed hungry—or left in coffin ships, and died—by the million ... If I've a sick pig—I want a pig powder, a syringe and farming papers, not some book about some knucks who don't matter any more. Anyway they're dyin'—all over the country—places like this ... It's starin' at them—a slate here and there—a few acres now and then—pressure—change—thirty—fifty years—that's all they've got—and men who understand how to buy and sell—who understand land and stock—move in—not for mouldy books, log fires—or wine ...

TRESSA *(Muttered)* To squeeze out "their own" ...

SCOBER For work!

TRESSA For nothing ...

SCOBER *(Ironically)* Must have been the way you were reared—this taste for the old style ...

TRESSA "Living", Barney—living ...

SCOBER   The homeplace—this bungalow your brothers
         built from a sixpenny plan—did you "live" over
         there? . . . *(Pause)* Plan must have said nothing
         about the dungheap . . . looks tidy outside the
         kitchen door—nice concrete walls, but . . .
TRESSA   *(Drily)* I was in Dublin when they built that.
SCOBER   I'd say . . . Couldn't see a book the last time I was
         there—a Sacred Heart and the butcher's calendar
         on the kitchen wall—that's the only style I saw.
         I wouldn't mind—only I gave you a free hand
         three years ago.

         TRESSA *nods impatiently.*

         Near a thousand pounds—that's what it was for
         paint and paper.
TRESSA   What's that when we end up with this—people
         who know about it think it silly —
SCOBER   What *people*?
TRESSA   The goldy wallpaper—the shiny lino—the prints
         —this bedroom stuff —
SCOBER   What *people*?
TRESSA   The ones last week—that's right—when I came
         back to the kitchen—I went down the back
         passage and listened. *(Pause)* Know what he
         said? "Hideous"—"Truly hideous" and then she
         said "I'd rather see it empty, open to the sky" . . .
SCOBER   I saw them . . . Who are they? He looked lek a
         man with a corkscrew up his arse, and she looked
         worried about it. Next time put the dog on them
         —I like it this way—the way you done it. *(He
         looks round the walls and ceiling: shrugs.)* If you
         don't like it now—we'll change it sometime . . .
TRESSA   I don't give a damn about it . . .
SCOBER   *(Nonplussed)* No?! Why all this whine . . . there's
         somethin'—what—?
TRESSA   *He* came back . . .
SCOBER   *Who* came back?
TRESSA   Maguire . . .

         Pause.

SCOBER   Here?

TRESSA *nods.*

TRESSA His cap—he said . . .
SCOBER *(Tensely)* Well . . .?

Long pause.

TRESSA He said—he saw you—years back: in a bad house . . .

SCOBER *reacts to this more with hatred of* MAGUIRE *than shame.*

Were you, Barney?

SCOBER *shrugs.*

With other women?

SCOBER *stares.*

You told me I was the . . .

SCOBER You're young . . .
TRESSA Were you?
SCOBER You don't understand . . .
TRESSA You lied.
SCOBER When you were born I was older'n you are now . . .
TRESSA I believed you . . .
SCOBER It was a poor question . . . and you?
TRESSA What?
SCOBER You?

TRESSA *stares suddenly distracted and embarrassed: pause.*

That's right: say nothin'—I'm a bit old for stories—what else?
TRESSA *(Embarrassed and angry)* What!
SCOBER 'Bout Maguire?
TRESSA *(Sharply)* I don't know—he talked in riddles.

SCOBER	'Bout me? . . .
TRESSA	And me . . .
SCOBER	What does he know 'bout you?
TRESSA	He can guess well — *(Pause)* "What's a woman for" he said, "scrape plates—twig floors, look at rocks and heather" *(looking back at* SCOBER*)* "To drain a man and rear a man" . . .
SCOBER	*(Almost in a whisper)* He said that?
TRESSA	More—he said—"Take me, I'm a man, I'll put a belly on you".
SCOBER	*(Incredulous)* You made that up?!
TRESSA	He said it . . .

Long pause.

SCOBER	"Put a belly on you" . . .
TRESSA	*(Deadpan)* That's what he said . . . *(Muttered)*— Maybe he could too.

Pause.

	You stand there as if nothing's happened— and . . .
SCOBER	*(With a great effort at control)* Nothin' did . . .
TRESSA	You don't care . . .
SCOBER	Why tell me this?
TRESSA	Because it happened.
SCOBER	A while back we made a deal—no talk—no half-talk—and you said *(Loudly)* Alright—and every day since—you give the jag,—your time—last night—Maguire—today . . .
TRESSA	I told you because . . .
SCOBER	"Reminded" me — because . . . *(Pause)* to-morrow—you'll let me know your time's up—the next day you're bitchy, the next itchy . . . You should travel with me and listen in—*you suffer* "How's all the care, Scober?"—"Any move on that woman of yours?"—"You want a *man* about the house". I listen and when they smile, I smile; when they laugh, I laugh, if a man's deaf—he's deaf . . .
TRESSA	You don't want to hear . . .

SCOBER   Hear what?
TRESSA   What you know . . .

Pause.

SCOBER   *(Tensely)* Say it! *(Pause; louder)* Say it . . .
TRESSA   You say it, Barney . . . you're not a proper man . . .

SCOBER *walks away:* TRESSA *goes to him.*

SCOBER   Leave me.

TRESSA   For God's sake, Barney—I didn't . . .
SCOBER   Thermometers — packages in the bathroom *(Pointing)* here and here—why don't you hang them up instead of these cheap pictures—and all these clothes, sponges—sprays—gadgets—pills? Where'd you learn it all?—at the Convent? In the Hospital?! I'd cut that hand off—here now—if I was told I'd . . .
TRESSA   "Get a cub *out* of me"—Keep your hand: adopt—it's easier . . .
SCOBER   What progeny? Sired by Maguire or his breed—that'd be somethin' to rear and work for—adopt! —that's what you'd get—worse maybe!
TRESSA   You can find out about . . .
SCOBER   No! No! *(Pause)* "Sweet as the September day they fell."

SCOBER *jerks his head in contempt; pause.*

TRESSA   It's hate you care about—not love—not me . . .
SCOBER   Nothin's happened? . . .
TRESSA   Even it did . . .
SCOBER   *(Stares)* It wouldn't be a story for me . . .

Pause.

TRESSA   *(Astonished)* You think I . . .
SCOBER   "A proper man"—That's what's in your head.

TRESSA You're raving . . .

SCOBER You rave asleep—in bed or out of it nothin' pleases you —

TRESSA *(Firmly)* I don't care what I say asleep—it's you I love . . . and . . .

SCOBER *(Loudly)* I'm not *blind* . . . *(Pointing down)* . . . Below I watched you—goin' 'bout with plates and teapots—lek as if you were stripped—on fire —they couldn't see it: I know you—Where's that yoke you'd on — *(He moves to the chaise longue, and scatters her clothes till he finds her blouse: he holds it by the elbow length sleeve—it shows dark sweat patches at the armpits)* You don't sweat for me like that . . .

TRESSA It was hot.

SCOBER *You* were hot . . .

TRESSA *(Her voice unsteady)* That's cruel, Barney—cruel . . .

SCOBER *during the latter half of this quarrel has rebuttoned his waistcoat and puts on his jacket again. He goes to the door and stands looking at her for a moment.*

SCOBER I know you . . .

TRESSA *(Bitterly, defiant, her voice unsure)* You know nothing—nothing—nothing . . .

SCOBER *stares and then goes out:*

(Calling after him) Nothing—nothing.

TRESSA *comes back distraught, the bitterness of many such experiences giving her control. She goes to the window and looks out. An engine starts below: car lights flicker—engine fades . . . she switches on the wireless.*

Drop down, or wheel on, set of a country store, illuminated by paraffin lamps. Half a dozen threshermen stand drinking at one portion which serves as a bar. The proprietor, TOBIN, is parcelling groceries for a woman customer, taking coins from one of the men, etc.

LYNCH *sits by himself, leafing through a paper at a small turf stove. There is a table near this, four or five chairs around it. As the curtain rises, it is clear that the men have been drinking and talking for some time.*

CONLON   The paper, Matt—what does it say?

LYNCH   'Bout what?
CONLON   Halpin's place.
LYNCH   *(Flicks through the paper and looks)* It's for sale.
CONLON   What does it say?
LYNCH   An ad—usual thing . . .
CONLON   Give it out, Matt.

> LYNCH *examines the ad for a moment and then reads, while he is reading* MAGUIRE *comes in, nods for his pint; exchanging winks and nods with the threshermen. He inclines his head to glean the information.*

LYNCH   "I have received instructions from the representatives of the late Peter Halpin, to sell at 2 o'clock, October 15th the following—His valuable farm, at Killnashallog, containing two acres three roods and twenty-six perches. Also one sixth share of Tormoncor mountain. The thatched house could be made comfortable for a small outlay. The out-offices comprise a stone piggery, and two-cow byre with a large concrete storage tank and an open turf shed. The garden comprises half a dozen young apple trees, and is rich and deep, consisting of lowland soil, carted in creels by generations of the Halpin family. There is a useful gooseberry patch. Subject to a half yearly payment to the I.L.C. of Two Pounds eight shillings and one penny."

Pause.

MAGUIRE   Gooseberries! . . . *(Brooding)* Squire Scober—The bad luck type! *(He shakes his head)* See the ghosty face of him at the head of the table and the cold monk's eye—all he needed on thon square head was a heather crown.

CONLON   If he gets Halpin's, he'll have all the heather there is, this side of the mountain.

TOBIN   A big wipe for a man with no childer.

CONLON   And poor sign . . .

MAGUIRE   *(Winking slyly)* But he knows the cure now, eh Charlie?

CONLON   What cure?

MAGUIRE   I told him a few weeks back; he didn't care about it . . .

MAGUIRE *sips his stout, deliberately for a moment.*

CONLON   Go on—go on Jemmy . . .

MAGUIRE   There was talk of childer here one night—you mind it, Charlie?

PUBLICAN *smiles weakly.*

PUBLICAN   I do.

MAGUIRE   Very serious, says I to Scober—there's a cure for your trouble—a sure one. Go back to your bedroom, draw the curtains, light a big log fire, have a basket of mud turf near, and get a table— on the table a bottle of the best Irish whiskey— then light a candle — *(Pause)* — and when you've done that — *(Pause)* — send for me!

There is loud laughter and nudging.

The bar door swings open and as SCOBER *comes in, there is a sudden silence.* CONLON *gives* MAGUIRE *an exaggerated elbow, and winks to the* PUBLICAN. SCOBER *sensing the source of their mockery, goes up to the counter with a deadpan expression.*

CONLON   You're back, Scober . . .

Long pause.

SCOBER   That's right.

39

CONLON What'll it be?

SCOBER shakes his head and nods at the PUBLICAN. *The men watch silently, aware of the tense glacial manner. The* PUBLICAN *puts a bottle of whiskey on the counter and a glass alongside it.*

SCOBER *(Glancing over at* LYNCH: *and pointing at the glass)* Another . . .

He takes out a large dealer's wad, and peels off a couple of notes. The PUBLICAN *puts up a second glass and holds out a couple of silver coins to* SCOBER *who points towards the mission box on the counter.* SCOBER *then takes up the bottle and glasses, and moves over to the turf stove. He puts them down on the table and sits down facing* LYNCH, *angled away from the bar talk,* MAGUIRE *watches the* PUBLICAN *put the change in the mission box and squints down to read:*

MAGUIRE Black babies—now you'd know that man was a good Catholic—it says here—that if you write to the Reverend Stanislaus Mulligan enclosing one pound, he will ensure that your entire name will be used to christen one of Africa's countless black pagans, What do you think of that, men?— "Wee black Scober MacAdam for £1 . . .".

LYNCH A cutty boy that.

SCOBER He does nothin', so he cuts the man that does.

LYNCH I don't like a mocker.

SCOBER Every clown's hobby in this country—a young man can stand it—he's got next year and the year after, and the year after to prove the mocker wrong; the aged man mocked goes mad . . . *(Pause)* . . . or less he finds the cure.

LYNCH nods and shrugs, SCOBER *pours two very large whiskeys.*

LYNCH *(Watching the glasses filling)* What cure?

Pause.

SCOBER   I bought well yesterday—we threshed well today, you've got to celebrate somethin' now and then, or you're dead before you get the chance.

LYNCH   I never seen this mix with *dalin'*—or anythin' for long . . .

SCOBER   Doesn't bother me—Here's profit . . .

LYNCH   *(Muttered)* Whatever that is.

SCOBER   Life, women in long dresses.

LYNCH   Is it?

SCOBER   If you can't get profit for yourself, you go somewhere and work for someone and you're what we were for hundreds of years—nothin'.

LYNCH   So they say—and if you get the knack of profit you want more and more—wasps round a jam-jar—is that life?

SCOBER   *(Pondering)* Women in long dresses, books, candles, wine, that's life! *(Pause) (Drily)* Says Mullarkey's daughter . . .

LYNCH   Your woman? *(Pause)* You'd know she was . . .

SCOBER   Mullarkey's daughter?

LYNCH   Schooled different.

SCOBER   Mercy nuns at Carrick—a few years in a Dublin hospital—that's not different when you're bred and reared like us. She's a country girl, not grand enough for tea the way they drink it in Foxrock, but a track too grand for the mug on the dresser. She has notions . . . a lot of notions.

LYNCH   A young woman doesn't settle for a while.

SCOBER *stares at* LYNCH: *Pause.*

SCOBER   Ah!

LYNCH   Takes her a year or two.

SCOBER   H'mm—you're not on these lines?

LYNCH   *(Laughs)* Me! What could I give a woman before . . . or . . . now . . . ?

SCOBER   Keep her settled.

LYNCH   The day's gone when you'd get a woman to live where I sold—no light or water—a paraffin stove, a mile to the mountain road—that breed of woman's gone.

Pause.

41

SCOBER	You've been with them?
LYNCH	*(On guard)* What way?
SCOBER	Bed? . . .
LYNCH	Well . . .
SCOBER	Clean or kip?
LYNCH	A journeyman listens, he has to, and I'm a close one . . .
SCOBER	That's why I'll talk—a man's got to be careful— you know—land in a kip—land in a clinic . . . *(Pause)*.
LYNCH	So they say.
SCOBER	So I know.

Pause: LYNCH *nods.* SCOBER *fills the glasses again.*

SCOBER	Can put a man wrong other ways—so's he's never right again—ever . . .
LYNCH	So they say.
SCOBER	So I know.

Pause: they drink again.

Some men don't—it's a thing to know *(Pause)* . . . Which?

LYNCH *looks at* SCOBER *and laughs.*

LYNCH	You're a curious man, Scober.
SCOBER	Well?
LYNCH	What odds? Today I threshed corn for you—next week I'm for the world.
SCOBER	*(Tensely)* I don't meet many men I like to talk with . . .
LYNCH	Nor me. *(Nodding at* SCOBER'S *glass)* You're empty.
SCOBER	What?
LYNCH	Your glass.

Pause.

SCOBER	Ah . . .

Pause.

SCOBER   These questions—I have a reason.

LYNCH   *(Shrugs)* 'S like confession, only there's no point.

SCOBER   I'll make your penance sweet.

LYNCH   *(Confused)* Tell what?

SCOBER   A journeyman with a thresher meets lots of women—what kind?

Long pause.

LYNCH   What matter?

SCOBER   It matters—to me . . .

Long pause.

LYNCH   *(Shrugging)* I never lay with kiphouse weemen.

SCOBER *pours another drink.*

SCOBER   Other kinds?!

LYNCH   That's my business—you've got thresher dust on the brain.

SCOBER   *(Fills LYNCH's glass)* What's the maddest kind of woman?

LYNCH   Don't know.

SCOBER   Guess.

LYNCH *shrugs.*

A woman who knits all day—and nothin' to knit for.

LYNCH   I'd an aunt like that . . .

Pause.

SCOBER   What do we work for?

LYNCH   In this country? Sweet shag all.

SCOBER   But *you* work—you jilt about with machinery—you stay alive.

LYNCH   To eat . . .

SCOBER   What else?

LYNCH   For what's over the hill . . .

SCOBER   The graveyard, son,—and the story no one knows

. . . But here on this mountain—what do we work for? bread, tea, buyin' and sellin'—the big cooker in the kitchen—the goldy wallpaper—eh? *(He shakes his head.)* We're dyin' steady every day— gettin' older, colder. No man minds the winter cold—cause Spring is comin' but if he got the notion that life went on: winter all the time . . . *(Pause)* You have to see young things comin'— light; growth, everythin', beginnin' again. That's what brings old men out to plough when they're not fit—or have no sons . . .

LYNCH H'mm.

SCOBER Do you folly?

LYNCH When they're not fit, and start to dote—*some* childer put them in the poor house—I've seen it . . .

Pause.

SCOBER When the time comes to dote and die—you're done anyway—what odds?

LYNCH I'd rather die with friends, than with tinkers in a stone ward.

SCOBER I'd rather not die at all—but if the finger points . . . *(He shrugs).*

LYNCH A man who knows how to live, and hates to die . . .

SCOBER An' for sure, won't be in the Litany of Saints . . .

LYNCH Who will . . .?

SCOBER *(Smiling)* You're a big honest lookin' fellow— you're clean—you respect women . . .

LYNCH I don't steal . . .

SCOBER You have to be educated to do that right— anyway, you're a Pilgrim—I hear you pray on mountains.

LYNCH When I'm afraid.

SCOBER Of what?

LYNCH The Devil.

SCOBER I meet him every day . . . in broad daylight—on the mountain—in the fairs . . . He's in this pub— he looks like that hooked nosed knuck over there . . .

LYNCH   Maguire?

SCOBER *(Nods)* He finds the weak spot and turns the knife till you act or go mad. An hour ago—after the grub—he went back—to talk to her . . .

LYNCH   Above?

SCOBER *(Nods)* To her face he said——"Take me, I'm a man, I'll put a belly on you."

LYNCH *screws round to look at* MAGUIRE.

LYNCH   She told you this!

SCOBER *nods.*

I'd kill a man for that.

SCOBER Not clever.

LYNCH   I'd break every bone in his body—dress him like a suck pig . . .

SCOBER No good.

LYNCH   But . . .

Pause.

SCOBER *She* said—"Maybe he could" . . .

Pause: LYNCH *drinks, pulling his nose.*

LYNCH   *She* said that?

SCOBER It's her *time*—so I said—to myself *(long pause)* Why not *a man*—the right man . . . *(long pause)* A man I'll pick . . . *(long pause).*

LYNCH   I'm not your man, Scober.

SCOBER You are.

SCOBER *pours the rest of the whiskey into their glasses, and beckons to* TOBIN *who brings over another half bottle of whiskey.*

TOBIN   Bit of a celebration, Scober?

SCOBER That's right.

TOBIN   A good yield, they say . . .

SCOBER *nods, and pulls out the large wad again, and peels off one.* TOBIN *gives him change and* SCOBER *leaves the wad on the table.*

	You could tempt a man with that . . .
SCOBER	I'd say.
TOBIN	A deal?
SCOBER	Kind of . . .
TOBIN	Who's buyin'?
SCOBER	Me . . .
TOBIN	What's between ye?
SCOBER	There's no price fixed—he's not sellin'—yet . . .

The PUBLICAN *looks from one to the other, shrugs and leaves. As he approaches the bar the dialogue around the bar becomes more audible.*

MAGUIRE	What's the deal, Charlie?
TOBIN	Scober has the cash—Lynch won't sell.
CONLON	Sell what?

TOBIN *shrugs.*

| MAGUIRE | What's he got to sell? |

TOBIN *shrugs again.*

TOMMY HAYES	Thresher . . .?
MAGUIRE	'S not his—co-op hired . . .
CONLON	Land?
MAGUIRE	Sold—he'd got nothin' that man, but notions and a big head.
CONLON	But Scober's buyin'?
MAGUIRE	Tryin' to buy.
LYNCH	They're watchin' . . .
SCOBER	When they're not you're nobody . . .
LYNCH	Put it away—it's no good to me.

SCOBER *takes the notes, looks at them, and puts them away in his pocket.* LYNCH *reaches for a half bottle of whiskey and begins opening it.*

46

SCOBER	Forbid a man: he steals—offer him and he shrugs —are you scared, son?
LYNCH	Not scared.
SCOBER	What so?
LYNCH	It'll tell after.
SCOBER	What will?
LYNCH	Conscience.
SCOBER	Yours or mine?
LYNCH	Both.
SCOBER	What's it to you . . . In a few days, where'll you be—on a boat half way across the world.

Pause.

LYNCH	*(This time* LYNCH *reaches for the bottle and pours)* Still makes poor sense.

Pause.

SCOBER	You come with me—now . . .
LYNCH	Above?
SCOBER	We can talk.
LYNCH	And then?
SCOBER	She'll come down—she always does.

Pause.

LYNCH	And then?
SCOBER	We'll *talk* like I said.
LYNCH	Talk . . .? How talk?
SCOBER	Nothin' sudden—she's no thick wit. I'll make the talk.
LYNCH	She's your woman—you know her . . .
SCOBER	*(Suddenly bitter and inebriate)* She's nobody's woman, and she's got secrets I know nothin' . . .

MAGUIRE *comes over holding a pint glass in his fist: he stands looking from* SCOBER *to* LYNCH, *swaying slightly.*
(Quietly) The Devil himself . . .

MAGUIRE	*(To* LYNCH*)* I don't know much about you, son— but whatever the deal, you'll be snigged by that

man there—and badly snigged. MacAdam's got a badger's head but he thinks like a fox—remember that—a fox.

SCOBER *pockets what's left of the whiskey, takes his hat from the table and moves towards the door.* LYNCH *stands up, looking from* SCOBER *to* MAGUIRE, *to the men at the bar, and then follows* SCOBER *out.*

SCOBER   There's rats in every ditch: night Charlie . . . men . . .

SCOBER *goes.*

MAGUIRE   What's he after, son . . .

Long pause.

LYNCH   Parcel of . . . bog . . .
MAGUIRE   He'll get you drunk, buy it for nothin'. If I was you, I'd stay away . . .

LYNCH *hesitates, then leaves.*

He'll buy your bit of a bog and bury you in it . . . deep.

Lights go out on bar set.

Curtain.

SCOBER *comes on stage (hall) and gropes for the light switch.* LYNCH *follows, and they stand listening. There is a radio upstairs somewhere.*

SCOBER Hallo . . .

Pause.

The radio goes off. LYNCH *shifts uneasily, and looks up at the D.C. lights which are pulsing faintly.*

SCOBER *(Looks up, listening)* Hallo . . .
TRESSA *(Offstage, above)* Alright . . .

SCOBER *nods and moves towards* LYNCH. *They both stand looking at the floor, listening to* TRESSA *moving about upstairs. After a few moments they look up together, catch each other's eye and move away.* SCOBER *moves towards a table and puts the half bottle of whiskey on it.*

LYNCH Scober . . .
SCOBER What?

Pause. LYNCH *looks up at the light for the want of something better to do.*

LYNCH *(Pointing)* Your lights—eh . . .
SCOBER *(Nodding)* Dynamo: I make my own light . . .

TRESSA *comes round the corner of the staircase, drawing the cord of her dressing-gown. She stops abruptly when she sees* LYNCH.

SCOBER You're alright—you know, Matt.

TRESSA *nods and stands looking down.*

We could eat . . .

TRESSA *nods again, and then comes on down the staircase, looking steadily at* SCOBER *and* LYNCH. LYNCH *nods faintly.*

TRESSA I was in bed—I didn't hear the van . . .
SCOBER You had the wireless . . .

Pause. TRESSA *and* LYNCH *stare at each other.*

TRESSA There isn't very much . . .
SCOBER We'll take what we get—cold meat—coffee—bread, anythin' . . .

TRESSA *nods and goes off. When she has gone* SCOBER *goes over to the sideboard and carries back two glasses and a jug of water.* LYNCH *sits sideways on a chair: his hands rubbing at his knees, unrelaxed.*

LYNCH She's eh . . .
SCOBER *(Pouring)* Yeah?
LYNCH Not just—a lump of mountainy woman . . .
SCOBER *(Stops pouring; reflecting)* She's a woman—like any other . . .
LYNCH But special . . . kind of.
SCOBER You're like a man waitin' to be shot . . .

LYNCH *takes his hands off his knees and straightens round to the table.* SCOBER *hands him a glass of whiskey.*

LYNCH Look, Scober . . .
SCOBER Drink . . .

LYNCH *drinks.*

LYNCH It's just . . .
SCOBER What?
LYNCH I don't understand . . .
SCOBER No—Give a cub a knife—what's the first thing he does?

LYNCH *shrugs, disinterested, watching the kitchen door.*

SCOBER   He carves his name on a desk, a tree, and when he grows to be a man, he journeys, works, earns, builds, to make a mark—'cause the days and nights are quick, and soon his name is chiselled on a stone — *(Pause)* There's poor remembrance in a stone.

Pause.

LYNCH   *(Unlistening)* Yea . . .
SCOBER   *(Introspective)* Nothin'—nobody—!

TRESSA *comes in with a tray and cold meat, cups, a loaf, butter etc. She puts down the tray and as she is about to leave* SCOBER *points to a chair.*

Sit . . .
TRESSA   I'm not hungry . . .
SCOBER   No?—Sit anyway—we'll talk . . .

Pause. LYNCH *rubs at his chin, and* SCOBER *stares up intently.*

TRESSA   About cattle dealing and farms?
SCOBER   Not cattle and farms . . .

TRESSA *sits down slowly.*

(To LYNCH*)* . . . Good luck . . .

They drink.

Matt here's for the world.
TRESSA   *(Nodding)* I know.
SCOBER   Be back rich in twenty years.
LYNCH   I'm not particular about money.
SCOBER   I know men like that; in the poor house.
LYNCH   If I get enough.
SCOBER   How much *is* that? What do you say . . .

51

TRESSA   About what?

SCOBER   About money . . .

TRESSA   It doesn't mean anything.

SCOBER   SEE! You're well met . . . *(Pointing to the wall)* Wallpaper three pounds a roll, doesn't mean anythin' 'cept three pounds a roll . . . *(Pause)* What age are you, Matt?

LYNCH   Thirty-two . . .

SCOBER   H'mm . . .

LYNCH   That's right.

SCOBER   *(Pointing to* TRESSA*)* She's twenty-nine—that's right? *(Pause)* And I'm fifty-nine . . . *(He looks from* TRESSA *to* LYNCH*)*.

LYNCH   That's not old—my old fella was over sixty when he married . . .

SCOBER   Over sixty?

LYNCH   That's right—and there were seven of us. I'm the youngest.

TRESSA   Where are they? . . .

LYNCH   Here, there, the States, New Zealand . . .

SCOBER   In the old days, people starved to stay here—to keep their names on the mountain. You have to fight to stay here.

LYNCH   If you want to . . .

SCOBER   The day I was born me mother died . . . I was dragged up by the auld fella . . . ignorant as they come he was . . . a drunk and a thickwit who hanged a stray dog he once caught worrying our sheep . . . when *he* died I was eighteen and that poor that . . .

TRESSA   Not that story, Barney.

SCOBER   Why not?

TRESSA   It's . . .

SCOBER   True, isn't it? I was that poor I couldn't truck with burial men . . . so I stripped him . . .

LYNCH   Your auld fella . . .?

SCOBER   Put him in a rain barrel at the back of the house, scrubbed him clean for his best night shirt and a chape coffin . . . scobed out a grave at night on my lone and hearsed him at day-light from our cottage to the church . . . in an ass and cart.

LYNCH   No neighbours offered help? . . .

SCOBER	Offers . . . but not offers I'd call offers . . . if you get me.
LYNCH	You're a suspicious man, Scober.
SCOBER	Have to be . . . *(Pause)* We're a mean breed up here. *(Pause)* Where was I?
TRESSA	Burying your father . . .
SCOBER	Oh aye. Thirty bob they gave for the repose of his soul and for all the mention then . . . or since . . . he might have never lived.

Daniel McAdam
Born 1873
Died 1932

	Born, died.
TRESSA	*(To* LYNCH*)* Do you want coffee?
SCOBER	"Matt"—His name's Matt . . .
TRESSA	*(Quietly)* I know . . .
SCOBER	Aye, Matt.
LYNCH	Matthew.
SCOBER	Aye, Matthew — . . . She's Tressa . . . Teresa! . . .

TRESSA *goes out: they watch her.*

SCOBER	Twenty-six on the clock when I got her—and never had a hand on her—bonnet never lifted—so she swears. But for a virgin she's well run in. Sits on secrets like a broody hen, and she has them . . .
LYNCH	You dream it . . .
SCOBER	Yesterday's fair was *yesterday*—and if I bought bad it's no comeback—no questions. I'll sell again or keep—but no questions. Ever see a woman buy?—They fret and fuss and folly every stitch—upside down: inside out—do everythin' but eat the bloody thing. They have to know—to get things on their list—so's they can forgive but not forget—and if you lie they'll catch you—and still they keep their secrets.

LYNCH *nods impatiently.*

(Noting his unrest) We're doin' well, son—sit . . .

	Give the thing time—we'll talk, drink coffee, and talk more—maybe after a while I'll disagree 'bout something and leave: when I do, you stay.
LYNCH	What time is it, Scober?
SCOBER	Well by twelve . . . one day short of Sunday.
LYNCH	You go, Scober?
SCOBER	Where?
LYNCH	Mass.
SCOBER	Do you?
LYNCH	I do.
SCOBER	She goes.
LYNCH	You go nowhere?
SCOBER	Christmas, Easter, Anniversaries . . . times like that.
LYNCH	You're not afeered?
SCOBER	Of what?
LYNCH	Could earn you Hell.
SCOBER	They'll burn quicker for their bad sermons, not but Peter Hannigan's a decent wee man. You know auld Peter?
LYNCH	Father Peter Joe?
SCOBER	That's him : comes up here twice a year. "Barney", says he to me once, "you're on the wrong track . . . You've got your values wrong". "You do the prayin' Peter", says I, "and I'll mind the values".

SCOBER *barks out a sudden laugh and then broods.*

Pity of an auld man like that: watchin' for his Maker and bullied, they say, by a niece that's watchin' for his money.

TRESSA *comes back, carrying a jug of coffee.*

SCOBER	There's a woman like you, Matt, religious. Why do you go, woman?
TRESSA	Where?
SCOBER	Mass on a Sunday.
TRESSA	Because . . .
SCOBER	Thinks same as me . . . went nowhere in Dublin . . . for a brave while . . . but goes here. There's a word for that.

TRESSA Not hypocrisy . . .

SCOBER What so?

TRESSA Something to catch at and think on forby life here . . . Hope . . .

LYNCH That's true, Scober.

SCOBER Words.

Pause.

SCOBER Know what I believe in my heart and soul . . .? When I die they'll put me in the ground and I'll stay there!

LYNCH Take a strongwinged angel to fly you up, Scober.

SCOBER Am I right though?

LYNCH Words . . . too . . .

SCOBER Poverised down half a thousand years, had to believe in what comes after . . . What else was there?

TRESSA *(To* LYNCH*)* You sold your farm?

LYNCH A bounds of rock and twisted trees—miles from anywhere.

TRESSA Do you have to live near a town to be happy?

SCOBER A man has a fight to keep his name on this mountain.

LYNCH Why not another mountain where the grass is sweet? . . .

SCOBER 'Cause you've got roots here: that matters.

TRESSA *(Muttered)* Whin roots.

SCOBER Did you hear the woman, Matt, did you? Whin roots.

LYNCH *nods.*

SCOBER I hear her all the time—she doesn't know how well.

TRESSA Where'll you go?

LYNCH Canada . . . States maybe . . .

SCOBER And every day you'll want to come back and plant spuds between rocks, turn wet turf, listen to a curlew . . .

LYNCH In rags, in the rain . . . not me.

SCOBER You're wrong . . .

TRESSA	Every man's different.
SCOBER	You'll come back . . . Your auld fella, Matt . . . was he any good . . . did he try?
LYNCH	I was reared by an Uncle.
TRESSA	Your people died?
LYNCH	Yes . . . good fiddler the uncle . . . travelled most ends of the country . . . ceidhles, fleadhs, firesides. Told me once he must have drunk stout in a thousand pubs and sung and fiddled near ten thousand songs . . .
SCOBER	He worked oddtimes?
LYNCH	Hard.
SCOBER	What went wrong?
LYNCH	He died last year.
SCOBER	Aye . . . but what went wrong?
LYNCH	What way, Scober?
SCOBER	You've sold your land, son . . .
LYNCH	Poor land's a rotten halter.
SCOBER	You name me somethin' that cuts closer to . . .
TRESSA	"We come from it . . . live off it and go back to it".
SCOBER	True woman and your dryness won't alter it.
TRESSA	You say it so often, Barney.
SCOBER	You say other things.

Uneasy pause.

SCOBER	I'll tell you what I'm comin' at, Matt. Your uncle, he had a place—you growin' into it—a poor pocket maybe, but *land,* yours, not a morning but you could look about you—the fields—the yard,—you know every gap and ditch and what grows on them. There's a white owl they say flits about them twisted trees that bounds Maguire's patch.
TRESSA	There's wild damsons in that scrub.
SCOBER	Great wee squirrel of a woman this: she has the cupboards stocked with jam and bottles from the garden: and gardens? What I'm sayin' if you've done things to land—red a field of stones say and buried them for drains—laid out an orchard or a

wood—it's done—it's there you can see it loam and bog and high bracken ground, sweet or sour, yours, to work with for a while and leave to . . .

Pause.

You'll come back.

LYNCH   It's no life *(Pause)*. The uncle that reared me, John Caffrey . . . he bought a field of whins, three acres of them—thick as your arm, roots the same, so he got a stubbin' axe, and he stubbed and cut and dug thousands of whins, followed every root under every rock, and burned as he cleared, sledged the rocks and dunged the ground. Three winters it took him—I helped him when I could.

Pause.

The first summer it was cleared he died mowin' hay off it.

SCOBER   *(With disgust)* Ah!

LYNCH   What?

SCOBER   That's it.

LYNCH   What?

SCOBER   The whinge and the whine about whins and rocks, it never quits *(mocking)* "And he died mowin' hay off it"—a poor bloody country all right—but it's a poorer breed of man lies under the like of that.

LYNCH   *(Stung)* He didn't lie, till he was dead—he worked—hard.

SCOBER   For nothin' . . .

LYNCH   *(Loudly)* That's what I'm tryin' to say . . .

SCOBER   *(To himself)* I tell you a man's got to fight to keep his name on this mountain, 'cause day brings night, brings day, brings death on any mountain, and the shadow has its time—only here they never work against it—they watch and wait and listen to what's preached and talk in ruts . . . *(moderating a little)*. A man doesn't live his life here—he waits for death, bites his nails and counts his sins. Hell burns all the time, so

57

why make friends or fields, or gather reeds for thatch that rots?—Stay or drift, it's all the same. Nothin' matters but the end *(pause)* and after . . . *(pause, he shudders faintly: with inebriate annoyance)*. But I say—let the cryers—cry. I'm a buyer—I'll *buy* and reckon later . . .

LYNCH   *(Drily)* That's right, Scober . . .

SCOBER *looks from* LYNCH *to* TRESSA *and pours more whiskey in his glass. Pause.*

SCOBER   Never lay with a woman—this man here—that's what he told me below—would you believe that? I don't.

TRESSA   *(Embarrassed)* They say Canada's good—a good chance.

SCOBER   Thirty-two and never lay with a woman . . .

LYNCH   *(To* TRESSA*)* I thought of it a lot.

SCOBER   I'd swear it.

TRESSA   The government out there gives grants for land—but it's tricky some way . . .

SCOBER   It's natural . . .

TRESSA   I have an uncle in Canada, he got on well.

SCOBER   It's natural.

TRESSA   You've too much taken.

SCOBER   When you fall off your feet you've too much taken—I never done that in my life.

Pause.

. . . He knows nothin' this man here—but this *woman* . . .

TRESSA   *(Interrupting with dull bitterness)* Barney! . . .

SCOBER   Well?

LYNCH   There's no harm in whiskey talk.

SCOBER   It says things—she's afraid of things.

TRESSA   I'm not.

SCOBER   Talks stupid—you've got to *say* somethin'—Canada—Christ!

TRESSA   *(Tensely)* Go on—say your things.

SCOBER   *(Refills the glass in his hand, staring)* I'll say I'm an aged man . . . *(Pause)* an' I've got a young woman—right?! (LYNCH *nods uneasily*) What does that add? (LYNCH *shrugs*) It adds up to a story—ever hear 'bout the old man went out to sow corn in a March field, and the young woman who carried for him? ... (*Pause*) He wasn't *fit* so he hired in this young man and all day long the young woman carried seed to the young man, and the field was sowed and harrowed—it grew well that summer, and they reaped it before the cold came—right? (LYNCH *nods:* TRESSA *stares impassively*) (*Suddenly cheerful*) Know what he can do? Lift the back end of a tractor himself.

TRESSA   My brother Willie can do that.

SCOBER   Aye—Willie's a slob—this fellow here has somethin' in his head. (LYNCH *shrugs*) He's a kind of saint—that right Matt?—like you—he prays; not all the time; fits and starts—tell her about Croagh Patrick, Matt—she'd like to hear about Croagh Patrick.

LYNCH *pushes his cup over for coffee. Pause.*

Sometimes he thinks there's a devil on this mountain and he sweats at night—can't sleep—can't work right—so what do you do, Matt? He throws all there and away for Croagh Patrick like some man a thousand years ago—night and day, eats where he can, sleeps in lofts or fields, then climbs this other mountain on an empty belly, and sits there all night, crouched up in the rocks in the rain—what happens then, Matt? Tell her what happens.

TRESSA   (*Defensively*) Mock a man—you mock yourself.

LYNCH   It's no odds.

SCOBER   Sits there all night—then down he comes; and gets *drunk*! That's what it is to be Irish: well I'm not that kind of man, and I don't mock this man, 'cause he's got everythin' a woman needs ... (*Pause*) 'Cept money—'course we have a deal comin' off, haven't we, Matt?

LYNCH   (*Dead pan*) Have we?

SCOBER   I'm buyin'—if you're sellin' ...

SCOBER *pushes a plate of cold meat towards*
LYNCH *who has just pushed away his plate.*

LYNCH   Not hungry.
SCOBER   You need it.

LYNCH *hesitates, and then takes a portion of sliced meat onto his plate.*

See that—honest young fella—eat off the other man's plate—doesn't bother him—holy sort of fella, Croagh Patrick, Lough Derg, Knock, Knock, Who's there? (SCOBER *laughs suddenly*) (*To* TRESSA) Take some coffee woman or you'll get a belly chill in this barracks—go on, pour, . . . warm up. —Talks in her sleep this woman.
LYNCH   So do I.

TRESSA *reaches for a cup and begins pouring coffee for herself.*

SCOBER   Walks in her sleep too—I got her one night here below at a big feed of bread and milk—didn't know where she was—the eyes goin' like taps—whining like a bitch in heat—that right?
TRESSA   There's no coffee . . .
SCOBER   Isn't it?
TRESSA   It's what you told me, Barney . . . I'll get more . . .

She gets up and goes to the kitchen, both men staring after her, LYNCH *stands up and moves about restlessly.*

SCOBER   Look at her and millions and millions this moment think it's somethin'. It's nothin'—like grub—mouthed in, and hunkered out—or anythin' that men and women do—an itch, a scratch, it's gone—means nothin'—nothin' less it grows to somethin' . . .
LYNCH   It's more'n that—(*Pause*)—we've had a lot . . . You can talk all you like, but sometime you'll have to say "this fella's goin' to bed with you".

SCOBER   *(Staring hard)* I knew it . . .
LYNCH   What?
SCOBER   You're scared . . .
LYNCH   I'm not a dog . . . You'll have to say it—or . . .
SCOBER   I'll say nothin'—I'll make her think it—and then
          . . . she's beginnin' to . . .

The door opens and TRESSA *comes in with a pot of coffee.* LYNCH *stares at her as she moves towards the table: they stand looking at each other.* TRESSA *puts the coffee pot down.*

TRESSA   You're going now?

Pause.

SCOBER   He's not—sit, son, it's early.

LYNCH *hesitates, and then sits down slowly.* TRESSA *pours him coffee, smoothing back her heavy hair from her forehead.* SCOBER *sensing an awareness between them, begins to act like a man trapped, looking from one to the other as though looking for a way out. Pause.* SCOBER *stands up swaying a little, drinks the coffee and puts down the cup.*

SCOBER   I've to go up here—a minute *(To* LYNCH*)*. If you
          say a thing mean it . . . if you make a deal . . .
          keep it . . .

He goes towards the staircase, and TRESSA *stands looking at* LYNCH*;* SCOBER *turns halfway up the stairs, looking from one side to the other, blinking, and running his tongue round his lips.*

(Still to LYNCH*)* Know what happened after we
left? *(Pause: to* TRESSA*)* Tell him 'bout Maguire—
he had a plan—tell Matt—he's young—he's like
a man'd listen—like a man'd understand.

SCOBER *stands swaying, as if about to say more,*

and then turns abruptly and goes up the staircase.

TRESSA He told you—didn't he?

LYNCH *nods.*

I knew from him; and you—whiskey makes him this way—it's not just me—all women. *(She shrugs).*

SCOBER *stumbles above and mutters.*

LYNCH You married him?
TRESSA *(Stares brooding)* He did things —

LYNCH *nods.*

LYNCH I'd say . . .
TRESSA Not just talk.
LYNCH *(Drily)* I know.
TRESSA *(Defensively)* He's always made other men seem —*(She glances at* LYNCH, *and hesitates)*—anyway —I didn't think of him as old—but as a man I'd like to live with, and get to know.
LYNCH Have you?
TRESSA A bit—he's mad jealous.

LYNCH *stares incredulously.*

He pretends not—but I know—we weren't married a week, when he started about young fellows—all bums, all useless, stupid "slobber gobs"—'specially if he saw them with a girl— and every month that passed he seemed greyer, wickeder somehow.

LYNCH I thought a jealous man was . . .
TRESSA A man who loves?

LYNCH *nods.*

In his own way—he does.

Muttering is heard in the bathroom; LYNCH *looks up and then walks over and examines a print hanging on the wall.*

TRESSA   *(Watches him and then indicating the hall and house)* This is all me—he's outside—the concrete —steel barns, rat proofed lofts, machinery sheds.

LYNCH   *(Glancing around)* Bare . . .

Meaning SCOBER'S *work, pause:* TRESSA *fingers the top button of her dressing gown.*

(Quickly) Outside I mean . . .

TRESSA   It's the trees.

LYNCH   What trees?

TRESSA   They're gone now—he called them *bushes*—he cut them down and blew out the stumps.

LYNCH   He's a business man . . .

TRESSA   *(Shaking her head)* So's the light could be seen at night—all over the mountain—it's like an asylum now. *(Pause)* But he gets things done.

LYNCH   H'mm . . .

TRESSA   Not just talk . . .

Pause.

LYNCH   Does he scare you?

TRESSA   *(Smiling)* Me . . . Barney—why? *(She shakes her head).*

LYNCH   Well—he gets—he does what he wants.

TRESSA   It's his place—his money.

LYNCH *looks hard at* TRESSA *and nods.*

Should that scare me?

Another noise upstairs.

The first day I met him he scared me—I was on accident duty, and he came in with his thumb half-hanging off—crushed in a lorry ramp—but he sat there as if he was waiting for an X-ray.

63

When we got him fixed up I found he was from my country. He came again—brought me through Dublin Mart one morning in the dark—I watched him—he could buy—saw him talk with dealers—shippers, auctioneers—I knew nobody like this—who'd ever bothered with me—a man who knew what he was doing and did it well.

LYNCH   H'mm . . . Business.

TRESSA   At home *(she shrugs)* they talked—I listened too long . . .

LYNCH   I know . . .

TRESSA   All winter long—about a drain—a ditch—building an out-house, or getting another sow—planting trees—it's never done—talk . . .

Suddenly restless again: LYNCH *looks up at the door, nodding.*

LYNCH   I know.

TRESSA   You're the first man he's ever—brought in . . . *(Pause)* like this—when there's a deal—it begins and ends below in the yard—I watch from the window.

Pause: TRESSA *waits for his answer.*

LYNCH   Whiskey—and I'm a journeyman—a stranger . . .

TRESSA   What is it anyway?

LYNCH   What?

TRESSA   This deal? He wants you to stand in—to buy or sell—land, stock, something?—To *use* you . . .

Embarrassed, LYNCH *is about to say something, when the bathroom door opens above—*SCOBER *comes round the staircase—they both look.*

SCOBER   Well? *(Long pause)* Looks nice down there . . . as it used to be—a woman in a long dress and a young man with a glass in his hand—that's life—says Mullarkey's daughter . . .

LYNCH *puts his cup on the table.*

              God be with the good old days and ways—we haven't the guts for 'em.

LYNCH   I think, I'll . . .

SCOBER   You'll not—you're a pilgrim, son—you'll stay here for penance.

LYNCH   It's late.

SCOBER   When it's light it's late . . .

SCOBER *comes down the staircase a little, staring from one to the other—again—the crazed, tortured, trapped, jealous look—which compels him to shatter his scheme, and throw the blame and bitterness on* LYNCH.

              There was talk—what?

TRESSA   I talked—he listened.

SCOBER   'Bout what?

TRESSA   This—that—nothing.

SCOBER   *(Violently)* I hate talk 'bout nothin'—if you talk, talk business, ask somethin', say somethin'. Tell him the way it is . . .

LYNCH   Scober, I . . .

TRESSA   *(Drily)* The way *what* is?

SCOBER   You, the way you know you're a woman every month.

TRESSA   *(Screaming)* Stop . . .

SCOBER   *(Shouting)* Tell him.

LYNCH   Scober . . .

SCOBER   'S the way she screamed—black under the eyes—doesn't need whiskey to sit in a frost—she's red hot—in her magazine rags. —That's what she's trying to tell you son, and every buck she sees—here I am—a woman.

LYNCH *says something unaudible to* TRESSA *who shakes her head.*

SCOBER   No means yes—and there's your man—do you hear me—your man? . . .

TRESSA *understands for the first time and looking with incomprehension from* SCOBER *to* LYNCH: LYNCH *attempts to say something to her, but she is gone before he can say it.* SCOBER, *on the staircase, seems momentarily exhausted, almost frightened. A long silence.*

LYNCH   *(Dully)* I'll go, Scober . . .

LYNCH *has started to move towards the door:* SCOBER *steps from the staircase to the hall after him.*

SCOBER   . . . I've more whiskey—maybe we . . .
LYNCH   I knew it below—it's no good.
SCOBER   *(With bitter cunning)* You did!
LYNCH   I said it . . .

SCOBER *getting loud again.*

SCOBER   You said yes.
LYNCH   No, Scober . . .

LYNCH *moves away from the table towards the door.*

     Even it worked—couldn't go right.
SCOBER   Then why are you here? Home and say your prayers son—it takes *men* to act out things—not monks—*men* . . .
LYNCH   *(At the door)* She cares 'bout you, Scober . . .
SCOBER   You're scared—son . . .

Pause.

LYNCH   Ashamed . . .
SCOBER   I'll not buy that—scared, it's in your face, scared—outside, and puke with it . . .

LYNCH *moves, opens the door and goes out;* SCOBER *shouts after him:*

They'll sing after you, when you're gone—"The Tame Colonial Boy", with the big head and no balls.

(SCOBER *runs down to the door)* Do you hear me?

LYNCH *goes out into the darkness. There is an inaudible exchange and then* SCOBER'S *voice shouting:*

You're not a man—do you hear me? —Not a man . . .

Sound of rain and muffled voices, then a starting and the engine drawing away. Then sound of heavy rain outside.

Grey daylight: LYNCH *approaches the front door, looks around, peers through, and then knocks. Silence. He knocks again. When he hears a door closing above he steps back from the door and lights a cigarette:* TRESSA *comes down the staircase, slowly goes to the door and opens it. Her face seems ravaged by the bitterness of a long night: black under the eyes.*
During this dialogue with LYNCH, *she answers him drily, watching with a bitter fascination.*

TRESSA The co-op man himself! . . . What do you want?

Pause.

LYNCH There's bags needed . . . Is eh . . . the Boss . . .?
TRESSA He left with you.
LYNCH I slept here last night on a loft.
TRESSA With mice?

Pause.

LYNCH There'll be men out there soon . . . I have to . . .
TRESSA Have you a licence? . . . Not for machinery . . . the other sort . . . the ones they have for bulls, boars, stallions . . .
LYNCH If you think . . .

67

TRESSA   (*Suddenly vicious*) You know what happens to unlicensed bulls . . . the Vet. comes and . . . (*she clicks her teeth*).

LYNCH   His idea, not mine.

TRESSA   You came here . . .

LYNCH   He kept my glass full for an hour and when he put it to me I thought he was drunk . . . jokey . . . or mad.

TRESSA   You came . . .

LYNCH   I was half cut . . . and . . .

TRESSA   You'd look well in the show ground with a prize card on your nose, smiling with Lord Leitrim. Did *he* get his hand on you, he likes to see what he's buying—likes to see progeny first—(*Pause*) He *was* buying, wasn't he? That's what he meant?

LYNCH *hesitates again.*

What's the fee for a well grown man—a few fivers? (*She laughs bitterly*)—Did you think I'd smile and wait for you upstairs—and if I did, that he'd have paid you down here? (*Pause; she stares at him*) He'd have killed you.

LYNCH   If I'd let him.

TRESSA   Oh! There is a bit of a *man* hid somewhere—why did he mock it . . .

LYNCH   Last night I got drunk—and tagged along with an old fool who's wife told me he was—mad.

TRESSA   —Burn that old fool: you'd have wise ashes . . . You got drunk with a *man* last night—not a nice man—but *a man.*

LYNCH   Alright.

TRESSA   Who'd buy and sell you ten times—who'd fit more in his life than you would in ten lives . . .

LYNCH   Good luck to him . . . Last night you didn't . . .

TRESSA   Last night I was being nice to someone going nowhere—country's full of them—journeymen who've sold their land, and snivel into stout about the cruel country. —It's not the *country*—it's the *men.*

LYNCH   And I was sorry for you.

TRESSA   Why me—why not the old fool in the rain—who's gone God knows where—to come stupid fair, half mad—why me? I'm not shifting about like an overgrown schoolboy, or going in a boat because some uncle died in a hay field . . . If I were a man could lift tractors and walk the country in a day, I wouldn't run from a woman. Matt is right: something you walk over.

LYNCH   You're a bitch alright.

TRESSA   Last night, he'd have stayed out or been in on business—the difference between the man and the messer . . .

LYNCH   I'm here now . . .

They look at each other with fascination.

These bags . . . where do I get them?

TRESSA   Bags?

LYNCH   Seed bags . . . I was hired to thresh corn, not dog a bitch in heat.

TRESSA *suddenly slaps and claws at* LYNCH: *when she bites him he pushes her away. She falls and cries:* LYNCH *watches and then goes to her and helps her up: they look at each other and then go behind the bales offstage.*

MAGUIRE *and* CONLON *come on as they leave.*

MAGUIRE   And the old dog watches.

CONLON   What?

MAGUIRE   What he's not fit for . . . last night with Lynch the steady Whiskey and the Wad . . .

CONLON   I saw them . . . some dale.

MAGUIRE   He's got nothin' that's any good to Scober, and if a man's got nothing, what's there to sell, eh? . . . We have him now Joady . . . and if it bites him to his grave there'll come no crack of pity *(pointing to himself)* from this man . . . My Lord of the Mountain . . . My Lord of the Sheep-flocks . . . My Lord of the Dark Marts . . . My Lord of the Cattleboats . . . My Lord of Clon-haggard . . . Clipped with his crown tipped side-ways on his auld hacked face. If he gets his heir we'll know it for some journeyman's bastard. That should choke his greed . . . cut his strut to size . . .

Pause. During the dialogue between MAGUIRE *and* CONLON *men and neighbours have been arriving in twos and threes.*

TOMMY HAYES — *(Examining a pitchfork shaft)* What's it stand for?

MAGUIRE — His name: he burns his name on what he's got . . . trusts nobody . . . and he's right . . .

TOMMY HAYES — I mark nothin' . . .

OLD JIM hUGHES — You've got nothin' to mark, Tommy *(Laughter)*. Ever heard about Tessie Madigan, men?

CONLON — Tell us, Jemmy.

MAGUIRE — Dublin's greatest whore. She went for a rest to Kerry and after a week or two round the lakes when she was at herself she remarked this big fella ploughin' a field . . . young he was . . . strong lek you . . . so she watched and when the field was done she saw your man pick up the plough and chuck it over the ditch . . . a minute later he flung the horses after it . . . "That's the boy for me", says she . . . so she goes up to him . . . "Do you know who I am?", sez she . . . "No", sez he, "I don't". I'm Tessie Madigan", sez she, "the greatest whore in Dublin". "And I'm Willie Fagan", sez he, "the greatest whore in Kerry. I've just ploughed the wrong man's field".

The threshermen enjoy this.

We've a long day ahead of us. In the auld days it was the flail across a plank . . . the winter long and plenty of talk . . . now it's this thing howlin' chaff and dust . . . combines, groups and co-ops . . . All for Scober and the go go men, and we're the corn they'll fatten on, we're the chaff they'll blow to Birmingham, for good if they get their way. There'll be nothin' here soon but Scobers, tinkers and tourists.

LYNCH *comes from behind bales preoccupied, walking towards the threshing mill:* MAGUIRE *goes to him.*

MAGUIRE How's the form, Matt?
LYNCH Alright . . .

LYNCH *nods to the other men and immediately begins flicking through defective bags: holding out the good ones.*

MAGUIRE You're like a man didn't sleep much.
LYNCH Rain.
MAGUIRE Rain?
LYNCH That's right.
MAGUIRE What rain?
CONLON Last night . . .
MAGUIRE Journeymen get wise too young—eh, Lynch? Live on whiskey and other men's dreams. Low land, mountain land, winter, summer, bed down in barns, lofts, and bars, see so many faces, hear so many stories, get so many offers—of one sort an' another—they get a sickner and quit the country. That it?
LYNCH *(Ignoring him, stands up with an armful of bags)* We'll make these do . . .
MAGUIRE What?
LYNCH That's three dozen.
MAGUIRE You're terrible busy, son.
LYNCH We've a lot to do . . . Get this off—you, Tommy—tie this back—we'll have to make a start.

The two men slide off the threshing mill and begin pulling the tarpaulin off: LYNCH *bends and gathers up the driving belt and shoves it at one of the men.*

LYNCH Line this . . .

The man puts the belt round the driving pulley of the mill and goes off stage.

LYNCH *(Calling)* Is she on? *(Pause)* Well? *(Off)* Dead on.

71

Pause.

LYNCH   Roll her . . .

Sound of the engine starting offstage, and the mill pulley spins the drum slowly: The idea now is to suggest a day's work by lighting . . . fade right down to twilight . . . LYNCH, now tending the bags, does not see SCOBER until he feels the tug at his jacket. SCOBER nods him away from the hum of the threshing mill. LYNCH takes his time finishing tying a bag, fixes a fresh one round the seed spout. He motions another man to take his job, and walks over to where SCOBER is waiting. The hum of the mill fades.

SCOBER   *(Looking at the thresher and pile of bags)* . . . You done well.

Pause.

LYNCH has an oilcloth and during this brief exchange, he keeps wiping at his fingers.

LYNCH   That's the end of it . . .
SCOBER   No bother?
LYNCH   *(Shakes his head)* No.

Pause.

SCOBER   You saw her?
LYNCH   I saw her.
SCOBER   Well?
LYNCH   Well what?
SCOBER   The story . . .

Pause.

LYNCH   What story?
SCOBER   Don't mouse me . . . son.

Pause.

LYNCH   She'll tell it . . .
SCOBER   You first.
LYNCH   She's your wife.
SCOBER   You tell me.

Some of the men look over.

LYNCH   *(Quietly)* You hired me to thresh corn—it's
         done.
SCOBER   I owe you.
LYNCH   Not me, the Co-Op . . . Pay now or later . . .

Pause: they stare at each other.

SCOBER   I drove away.
LYNCH   You saw me walk away.
SCOBER   There was light—I watched it from the rock . . .
         All night I watched.
LYNCH   You owe fifteen quid.

Pause; TRESSA comes on.

SCOBER   She must've said somethin'.
LYNCH   *(Moving away)* She's your woman—ask her.

*During this exchange the men about the threshing
mill are putting the tools together in a bunch and
putting on their coats. They push the bales and the
bags of seed off stage. It is now almost dark.
LYNCH and TRESSA exchange looks. LYNCH goes.*

TRESSA   How did it go, Barney . . .?
SCOBER   It's finished.
TRESSA   Good as last year?
SCOBER   Better.
TRESSA   So we're set for the winter—tons and tons, let
         the criers cry outside the gates. We could shut
         ours and live well from the garden—barrels of
         bitter apples down there—but it's a dark time
         winter—lonely—'course we can dig a little on the
         short bright days, only the garden's like a
         graveyard . . .

Pause.

And you hate graveyards and gravestones—"Who was this man McIntyre, McInerney, McAlvanney, McElvinney, who are they; all these buried men?"

Pause.

	(Screams) Why?!
SCOBER	You lit fires round me night and day . . .
TRESSA	To think I'd sweat in bed with any slob you'd pick, and have a bastard with your name tagged on, and you to watch me grow, and know and not pretend, and when the cub was in the cot, stick out your chest proud as a bicycle pump!
SCOBER	I meant it for you, woman.
TRESSA	For Christ's sake, man . . .
SCOBER	Why not!? Tinkers in a ditch . . . dogs . . . bats and sewer rats . . . everything that runs, swims and flies can throw a likeness but us . . .
TRESSA	You've never loved . . . stay or go . . . me or you . . . it doesn't matter now . . . all night I thought of this . . . so I did it.
SCOBER	Did what?
TRESSA	What you wanted . . . with Lynch . . .
SCOBER	You're lying . . .
TRESSA	No . . . that's right . . . stare 'till your eyes burn out . . . you're blind anyway . . . *(beginning to break)* Don't you know why? . . . To reach you . . . not fool you . . . God I . . . can you not see . . . know . . . feel . . . how I loved you . . . yes, . . . loved you *(she breaks)*.
SCOBER	I meant it for you, woman.
TRESSA	For yourself, man . . . For respect . . . To shut Maguire and a gaggle of mockers . . . that's the truth and you know it, and I know it . . .

Pause: faint mocking laughter offstage.

	and *they* know it . . .
SCOBER	*(Almost incoherently)* . . . Dig out the badger . . . blind him with lime . . . jeer and cudgel . . .

split his belly . . . spike him to a tree, or any man that cuts his way up from what *they* are to what *I* am . . . That's their religion . . . Well by Christ I'll not be fed to scaldcrows . . . I'll bury every last man of them . . . I'll out-buy . . . out-crop . . . out-credit . . .

TRESSA Barney! You've lost . . . it's over.

Long pause.

We're not yesterday people . . . we're alone.